Durations

Durations

Poems by Herbert Scott

Louisiana State University Press

Baton Rouge and London

1984

Copyright © 1984 by Herbert Scott
All rights reserved
Manufactured in the United States of America
Designer: Barbara Werden
Typeface: Linotron Aldus with Palatino
Typesetter: Moran Colorgraphic Incorporated
Printer and binder: Thomson-Shore, Inc.

The author is grateful for permission to reprint certain of these poems, which have appeared in the following publications: "Old Woman in the Desert," *Cutbank 5*; "Fathers of Desire," *Fiction International*; "Early Love," *Great Lakes Review*; "Woman with Pitcher," *Green River Review*; "The Man Who Would Be a Mother," "Achilles' Heel," and "Travelers," *Mississippi Review*; "As She Enters Her Seventieth Year She Dreams of Milk" and "The Other Life," *Nimrod*; "Summer Storm," *Northwest Review*; "The God That Keeps Us Alive," *Passages North*; "Oklahoma Sunset" and "On the Missouri," *Poetry NOW*; "Dinosaurs" and "The Woman Who Loves Old Men," *Quarterly West*; "In New Mexico," *Red Cedar Review*; "The Fear of Telephones," *Skywriting*. "The Pact," copyright 1974 by Washington and Lee University, is reprinted from *Shenandoah*: The Washington and Lee University Review, with the permission of the editor.

The author wishes to thank Western Michigan University for two summer fellowships, during which a number of these poems were written.

Library of Congress Cataloging in Publication Data

Scott, Herbert.
   Durations.

    I. Title.
PS3569.C624D8 1984   811'.54   83-14947
ISBN 0-8071-1149-X
ISBN 0-8071-1150-3 (pbk.)

For Ann, Sue, Addie Lou
For Shirley

Contents

I Departures

Achilles' Heel   3
The Woman Who Loves Old Men   3
Fathers of Desire   4
The Dead   5
The Pact   5
Travelers   6
The Past   7
Old Woman in the Desert   7
In New Mexico   8
The Future   9
The Fear of Telephones   9

II These Poor Excursions

Stones   15
Dinosaurs   16

III Reconciliations

The God That Keeps Us Alive   43
Early Love   44
Summer Storm   47
Oklahoma Sunset   48
Woman with Pitcher   48
On the Missouri   49
The Ceremony of the Ducks   51
The Man Who Would Be a Mother   55
As She Enters Her Seventieth Year She Dreams of Milk   55
The Old Man in His Decline   60
The Other Life   61

I *Departures*

Achilles' Heel

The foot slides open, disjointed
toes askew, arteries spurting
legions of Greeks, Romans, the tribes
of Israel, Alexander, Hannibal,
and the long river we call *Helen*.
And the river rich with bodies, little flags
of hands protruding, the baby Moses, silt
that builds deltas at the mouth of darkness.

And the foot marking the throat of the slave
for the axe, for the hand to lift
the unencumbered head,
for the fingers never to be free again
of that wrath of hair.
The four-clawed foot
digging its terrible furrows. . . .

Or the slender, high bridge,
lacy, intricate arch, the lover's mouth
laid against the instep,
that curve of air, delicate slippage
along the long slip of thigh . . .
until all collapse
as the heel comes down,
shatters, as cities splinter,
as the foot turns, disembodied,
almost its own master.

The Woman Who Loves Old Men

She loves the brown moles
widening to pools of oil
on their faces, their eyes
turning to milk, the tiny
forests of their ears;

and the shoulders,
wearing thin as skulls,
the slow glaciers of flesh
sliding from bone;

and oh the white bellies,
the pure salt of their bellies,
she could bury her face forever
in such perfect snow.

Yes, she marries them,
and they roost in her arms
like tired birds as she listens
for the last drawn croak
before that certain stillness.

And they, thankful, never know
it is their deaths she loves,
their bodies she lays out
like polished wood, as she dreams
of the one who will marry her twice.

Fathers of Desire

We are fathers of the child
at its mother's breast,
the child who sleeps
in our doubled arms,
heavy and sweet.
This is a love we bless.

We are fathers of the child
on fire, who bears
no lips, no nose, no hair,
whose eyes will never close;
and fathers of desire.
No. We cannot forgive ourselves.

We are fathers of the child
who turns to stone, no heart
to moan into our ears
laid like flowers
against its chest. No one
loves us more than this.

The Dead

It is the dead who are always with us,
handsome and winning, on their best behavior.

We carry them in our chests
like an extra heart.

Companions who never falter,
who live in us their second lives.

And how can we deny them?
We who held them in our laps too long,

their languorous arms about our necks,
the breath of their sweet skin swarming.

How can we say:
This is the last kiss goodnight?

We who do not yet know
forgiveness was never possible.

The Pact

Our arms rest on the oak table like loaves of bread,
a sour smell of dough rising, the stink of ferment.
The table is old and marked by the black burn of an iron,
like the imprint of a hand or a club foot, our coat of arms.

We join hands, dividing the table,
each in his own sector, our fingers knotting in the center,
the body of an octopus. We are caught by the tentacles
of our own arms, taken by the shoulders like small children.
We admit we have drunk too much wine. No one remembers
why we are there. We shake loose, fall away like leaves,
the table tightening to a circle, a noose.
We pledge never to return, to brook no survivors.

Travelers

Who speaks in these cartoons
where the precipice
is simply a line
drawn off the page?

The flesh
is no harbor for joy.
It falls from us
like loose change.

Father, where
is your stern look?
Mother, your breasts
have flown away.

There is a distance
we cannot travel
between our hands
and the faces

of those we love.
Turn back, before
it is too late,
the girl screams

but the travelers
do not hear,

for the wind is blowing
her words into sky

as the camera swings
for a view
of the precipice
we anticipate.

The Past

We dreamt we nailed its coffin shut.
Awake, we know it waits for us
in the rooms of our deepest seclusions.

And we have learned nothing!
Not how to keep ourselves alive,
no hocus pocus . . .

When it slips into our beds, a former
lover, we feel how unfamiliar its skin is.
Yet we make love as if it were alive.

Again we know how all things fasten.
We have so much to say.
It will not listen.

Old Woman in the Desert

Her arms are dead rainbows
holding neither light
nor dreams. The sun

is no husband of hers.
Her hands stiff as antlers.
Her breasts dry washes.

Drunk, on your way home
from dying, you would not
sleep with her.

You would pass her by
like the dead mother
of your dreams

who sulks
in a stone chimney
somewhere in Oklahoma.

But you will remember
her eyes, petrified fish
in an ancient ocean.

You will carry them
in your pocket.
An atonement. A last rite.

In New Mexico

The road rusts
away. I follow
the yellow sandstone ridge
edging the sky.
In this desert
the past is a mirage
you almost believe in,
almost remember
from the last time
you entered your wife,
the heat welling up
like water
you would dig for
in the dry sand.
You scan the horizon.
Is it the rider
you look for, a fleck

in the lens of your eye,
hellbent forever?
Later you discover
the white ribs
of his horse, read
the scripture of his death,
witness to your own
private betrayal.

The Future

Ignorance, our bloody
scribbled child, casts off
swaddling clothes,
struts naked in boiling skin.

The Fear of Telephones

i.
The voice crackles,
lost somewhere
out there. We know
not to send
retrievers. All
they would find
are bones clicking
among themselves,
the wind picked clean
of all desire.

ii.
He is breathing
heavily,
his iron lung
keeping him alive.
She listens

for the first words,
knowing them by heart.
As if from under water
they bubble
into her ear
the message
she was born to hear.

iii.

Sometimes under
the spell of need
we receive all
that is given
to us, rejecting
nothing, our bodies
vibrating with hellos,
are you theres,
are you sure this
is a wrong number?

iv.

The deaths that pour
out, if we could
see them, how
they take their places,
climbing into any
chair, the unmade
beds. They say,
move over, we've come
to stay.

v.

The girl
with the broken neck,
the black hand,
the insane scream,
the innocent bystander,
the twitching eye,
the house burning
down around us.

vi.
If I could put
my hand down,
bury it in the ground,
let it take root
and live of its own accord,
I would still
feel those fingers
tremble, lay my ear
to the earth,
listen for your call.

vii.
If we can overcome
distance, the voice
traveling for centuries,
summoning other galaxies,
if it can live
beyond our own
reckoning,
who can say
it is not the soul
calling its own name,
all we have
of permanence.

II *These Poor Excursions*

Stones

I have one
dug out of a quarry
in the Parish of Cornwell
and given me by the ingenious
Sir Thomas Pennyston,
that has exactly the Figure
of the lowermost part
of the Thigh-Bone *of a* Man
or at least of some other Animal.

It seems to have been broken off,
shewing the marrow within
of a shining Spar-like *Substance*
in the hollow *of the Bone.*
In Compass near the capita Femoris
just two Foot,
and at the top above the Sinus
about 15 inches; in weight,
though representing so short a part
of the Thigh-bone, *almost 20 pounds.*

This Stone of ours
must have been a real Bone,
now Petrified.
It must have belonged
to some greater animal
than either an Ox or Horse;
and if so in probability
it must have been the Bone
of some Elephant, *brought hither*
during the Government of the Romans
in Britian.

   Robert Plot, First Keeper
   The Ashmolean Museum, 1677.

Dinosaurs

>On the Weber River in Utah
>July, 1977

On these shores
dinosaurs lay down to die
70 million years ago.

Their bones are stone
driven into stone.
It is dusk.

I sit on the ground
at the water's edge
writing these words.

Two boys in waders
fish beneath the low, curved bridge
downstream. Yesterday

they caught twelve bass,
threw them back,
the largest three pounds.

Today their luck is better.
What are you doing, they ask.

Broadleafed grass
grows in random clumps
among the stones.

The water is a voice
that cleans my bones.

*

> "You have found the remains
> of an animal new to science."
> —GIDEON MANTELL

A young woman walks
along a country road
in the Cuckfield district

of Sussex, while her husband
calls on a patient
dying of childbed fever

on an early spring
afternoon in 1822.
The woman pauses

at a pile of roadmetal,
bends down,
closes her hand

around a tooth
thick as a wrist bone
embedded in Tilgate stone.

I think of this
as an act of love,
Eva Mantell

affixing her small hand
to the tooth
of a dinosaur

lifting it from the earth
a gift for her husband
walking to meet her

from the bed of another woman
dying in the afternoon
sunshine of Sussex.

*

This afternoon,
after driving all day

across the dry wash
of Colorado and Utah

I came upon this river
among the low hills,

narrow and swift,
harrowed by stones.

I shed my clothes and waded in,
lowering my body

into the channel.
The cold, fast water

seemed to startle me alive
again, taking my body down

the river, glancing
against rocks. I threw

my head back, laughing,
beating my arms

against the water,
laughing at my own

strange body,
featherless,

scaleless,
ground-blessed creature.

*

I came upon a woman
kneeling on the bank

washing her clothes,
her breasts rocking.

She leaned on her haunches,
looked at me and laughed,

now lifting her long
red hair like water

in her hands,
catching it behind her ears.

I laughed again, at her beauty,
at myself, and was not shy.

*

Later, lying back
on the grassy bank,

I watched the woman
lift her skirt

between her legs
tuck it at her waist

until it billowed
around her thighs

like bloomers. She waded
into the water

shaking her hair
loose, a red shower

across the belly
of the late afternoon sun

the sky stark blue
above green and brown hills.

And the stones kept
their perfect peace.

    *

Three hundred years ago
John Lightfoot, Vice Chancellor
of Cambridge, announced

the date of Creation:
September 17, 3928 B.C.,
nine o'clock in the morning.

Archbishop Ussher of Ireland
preferred
October 23, 4004 B.C.

Now we need the earth to be
four billion years old, at least.

What can we know
in our insatiable ignorance?

    *

Here were dense swamps,
water lilies, horsetail rushes,
cypress, eucalyptus, fern.

On high ground, grape, laurel,
oak and sequoia, ebony,
bayberry, honeysuckle, ash.

Some lived in the marsh, thunder
lizards, fifty tons of flesh and bone,
heart the size of a woman,
bodies too heavy for dry land.

These were plant eaters,
duck-billed, bone-headed, beaked,
some with two thousand teeth,

tearing plants from the moist earth,
swallowing whole bushes,
young trees, rocks still clinging
to clods of soil around roots,

swallowing the rocks,
as much as a bushel of rocks
riding in the hold of the huge belly
grinding the plants to mulch.

Others lived on dry land,
lizard-hipped, meat eaters,
standing on two legs, swift,

powerful, some with skulls
six feet long
jaws strong enough to tear
whole limbs from live victims.

And all would grow back,
tree, vine, bush,
tendon, bone, flesh,

for 150 million years
all would grow back.

*

In 1802, Pliny Moody
found tracks in red sandstone

believed to be those of a large bird:
Noah's raven.

And few would believe
the real miracle of bones
hauled from the earth.

Sports of nature.
Fabrications of the stars.

Working models:
practice for the Creation.

False, fearful bones,
hoax of an angry God
to frighten us into belief.

Yet a sheep herder in Wyoming
built a small cabin
entirely of dinosaur bones,

and others, farmers,
miners, railroaders,
finding these bones,

took them into their homes
as ornaments, door stops,
playthings for their children,
and were unafraid.

*

Each summer I travel west
along these highways

from Michigan to California
to see my children.

In Fresno, the buildings turn
their weathered skins to the sun.

Del Webb's new townhouse
already closed down.

I remember a worker tumbling
to his death, thirteen years ago,

the year I moved east
to a different life.

Madame Temple
still reads cards on the corner

of McKinley and Wishon.
I remember too well

her legend:
There is no pity

for those who need help
and do not seek it.

*

Gideon Mantell, I see you
digging your way for years
through secret quarries,

giving up the living
for the dead

bringing the dead
bones back, your patient hands
peeling the limestone

flesh away, until those bones
seemed to breathe
beneath the ancient, sweat-stained dust.

Each night you kept your vigil
until the sudden light
of dawn startled you.

Or perhaps you heard
Eva
turn in her sleep

and you lay down
beside her, for a moment,
surprised at her warm skin.

*

Last summer, leaving
the dry heat of the valley,

my youngest daughter and I
drove to the coast, Pismo Beach,

the wind cold off the ocean.
We walked along the edge

of the surf that washes in,
covering our feet and ankles,

looking for shiny rocks and shells.
I looked down at the sand

patterns on my daughter's back
as she bent to pick up a shell.

A good one.
She put it in my pocket,

heavy with the day's collection.
I laid my hand outside the pocket,

feeling the weight of it,
the sun going down,

my daughter beside me, the sand
giving beneath our feet.

*

Waterhouse Hawkins
fathered the first
dinosaurs, in 1853,

great horned monsters
resurrected from the deep
grasses of England.

Half a century later
Othniel Marsh would say

*there is nothing like unto them
in the heavens, or in the earth,
or in the waters under the earth . . .*

But they were true
children
of this world

the mortal imagination
giving birth
to those transfigured beasts.

*

The boys wade
into the current.

Their arms snake out,
draw back, their voices

now and then

an indistinct music
above the water.

They must have been beautiful,
long, sinewy necks

muscle and bone
stirring beneath skin

the skin shining
like a morning dream.

*

Along the highway
from Colorado

into Utah, cement
and stucco monsters

rise from their deaths
in front of curio stands

pink, purple, polka-dotted
skins, feeble grins

no terror, no beauty,
no belief.

And we have watched
across the earth

these great beasts rise
from celluloid seas

or in our homes
become

fists of light,
these poor excursions

our desire to know,
their loss, our loss

our names written in stone.
If we are afraid

it is for the drowse
of our lives

in which these dreams
may die.

   *

At suppertime,
across a small meadow,

the red haired woman bends
above her camp stove

bushes and branches
of trees about her

laden with bright clothes.
She looks up, smiles.

A man claims her,
circles her with his arms.

I turn away. I am lonely,
my wife asleep

in her warm body
two thousand miles away.

Later that night
she will come to my tent,

lie beside me, take
my hands to her body.

I smile at my foolishness
and sit down to supper.

      *

You are still with me
after twenty years,
old woman, chanting

your story to Cunegonde
and Candide, on the way
to the new world.

You were taken
by a pirate captain
at fifteen,

your lover dead
in Massa-Carrara
of poisoned chocolates,

your mother, alive,
hacked to pieces
before your eyes.

You survived the plague
in Algiers, were sold into slavery,
raped a thousand times.

The starving Janizaries
who held you captive
during the seige of Azov

carved up
one of your buttocks
for food.

Growing old
in misery and shame,
only half a backside,

you say, *a hundred times
I wanted to kill myself
but I still love life.*

*

On New Year's Eve
at the Crystal Palace

twenty-one scientists
sat down to dinner

within the belly
of a dinosaur

a celebration!
Mantell's *Iguanodon*

the creation
of Waterhouse Hawkins

out of 600 bricks
650 half-round drain tiles

900 plain tiles
30 casks of cement

90 casks of broken stone
100 feet of iron hooping.

*

Why do we so love the body?

We carry the body within the body,
its small heart beating.

And then it comes.
And then it runs away.

Each year the gift
diminished

the darkness within
seeping through the skin.

Even after death we try to save the body.
The body in our arms.

Its well of breath gone dry.
The body in its disgrace.

*

This morning at the diggings
near Vernal

where 300 tons of bones
have been taken from the earth

I studied the remains
of fourteen dinosaurs

chiseled into relief
on the tilted face

of the quarry.
A woman in a blue dress

lifted her young daughter
to stroke a pelvic bone.

30 tons, brain
the size of a kitten's.

77 inches from sole to scalp
I could curl up

inside that bone, become
its stone child.

*

How we desire the earth
to open and yield
those great bodies

full-fleshed and lovely
in the glint of the sun

for them to come back
to what they knew

not to be held captive
in preserve or sanctuary

but to live beside us
and we beside them
living in wonder.

Only the possum knows.
Ancient and slow

like a favorite grandfather
who no longer speaks

he waddles along
crossing the road
into the weeds.

*

In America,
Waterhouse Hawkins

raises his studio
in Central Park

to house the birth
of dinosaurs.

He will set them free
in that wild habitat,

a gift to the people
of New York City.

Somewhere beneath
that unredeemed wilderness

those half-formed monsters
keep.

*

And I had forgotten
the blackbirds,
white-winged,

as large as grackles,
the most beautiful
I have seen.

All evening
I watched them along
the river, going

about their lives.
They are not scavengers.
They are not afraid.

They land beside me
as if there were a pact
between us. Perhaps

they like to watch me.
Perhaps I am beautiful
to them, as they are to me.

Or at least amusing.
When the blackbirds take flight
the white markings

of their wings
flare and disappear
like hands among clothing.

*

How can the body survive?
At night the hills receive
a different life,

texture changed to shadow.
Huge, stable bodies,
and what remains is form.

*

Nine teeth, a lower jaw,
bits of the upper,

28 vertebrae, the bones
of fore and hind limbs

dug from a marl pit, in 1858,
near Haddonfield, New Jersey

the first partial skeleton
unearthed in America.

Waterhouse Hawkins
married the bones

to plaster, to each other,
the head his own

invention. Waterhouse,
they broke these bones

down, in 1940,
laid them out

in a small glass case
in Philadelphia.

*

A car climbs the road
through the trees.

All I can see
are its headlight beams
tugging at the sky.

The boys pack up their gear,
wave good-bye,

walk from the river
to the road

the light coming down
from the sky

leveling, catching them
for a moment in its eye.

Now they are gone
with their luck

and their fish
and their slick wet boots.

*

The dinosaurs died
in a geological instant.

*A huge comet
loomed past the sun*

*sweeping the earth
with its tail.*

*Stinging insects.
A great ice age.*

*The earth rose up
and the marshes drained.*

*Nothing to eat.
Nothing to eat.*

*Primitive mammals
sucked their eggs dry.*

They lay down like bathers
after a long swim.

*

And you, Gideon Mantell,
died alone in a house full
of bones, in London.

Eva had left you.
Not enough room
in that house of bone.

The earth laced with bones.
Clean, cold bones, coming apart.

*

Here we are, singing
this mad opera

the story the usual
melodrama

the saving grace
of earthly music.

*

Who will name us?
How will we be known?

Will some life form
lift us from the earth
love our puny bones

these sticks
that won't bring fire,
carve them

into implements, ornaments,
unfold these arms
crossed against our chests

as if we could
hold in
death?

*

I am alone
with the river.

The moon,
a cup of light.

The working water
will not rest.

Something downstream
catches my eye,

comes slowly
towards me,

rising and falling
in the half-light.

Something alive
is all I know,

climbing the river.

*

Now I see
the muskrat

tail flashing
above the water,

disappearing, something
held in its mouth,

her young in her mouth.
She doesn't notice me

as she climbs
belly over stone

intent against the pull
of the river, the water

sucking her fur.
Primitive, essential

motion, learned
through centuries

of survival,
ordinary and beautiful

blood and bone
and wet fur.

*

She passes within
my arm's reach

her body gleaming,
leaping, dipping.

I could touch her,
the wet, sleek body,

but I would not.
For a space I have become

invisible
to other creatures.

*

There is a beauty
that rises from bodies

indescribable!
mingling with air and darkness.

We are its familiar gestures,
its words already spoken.

*

The water seems spun
to a delicate fiber
pulled over a loom

words only a memory
already distant

water spinning its way
past the muskrat

lugging her young
up the river.

She disappears, the night
too dark to see

these words
pushed across the page.

    *

I stand up
beside the water
and think of my wife

remembering
that summer morning
we walked

on the dark beach
at Pine Point, Maine,
before dawn,

wanting to see
the sun rise
above the Atlantic,

the sand cold ashes
beneath our bare feet.

We strolled,
arm in arm,
near the water,

looking out
to Prout's Neck

where Homer stood
in the flung surf

painting the pure fury
of our beginning.

*

I leave the river
and walk back to camp.

I can hear voices
again, laughter,

fire breaking wood
into coal and ash.

I crawl into my tent,
settle down among covers.

This small space is enough.

Kalamazoo, Michigan
May, 1978

III *Reconciliations*

The God That Keeps Us Alive

i.
Love, in whose honor
we grow towards the sky

in whose service
we diminish death

Love, on whose journey
we map ourselves,
the bodies of our mates

husband the grassy fields
where we feed
the pools where we swim

the shoals of bone
where we draw shelter

Love, we bend
to kiss you

becoming gods ourselves,
though not gods, and dying.

ii.
We mark our ascent
in kitchen doorways

in our children,
their shoes empty
as our lives would be.

Winter comes.
Trees die in this season

fall in the deep snows
unseen, unheard.

Beneath our feet
the earth shudders.

iii.

Love, brief father
who leaves us
orphans in dry rooms

winter heat
cracking our bones . . .

We are warriors
of loss

falling
in the streets
of foreign cities.

You lick our wounds,
the salt healing,
the blood remembering.

iv.

Love, you are
nearly great enough.

The myth you father
is worth the living.

Early Love

for Emma

Your skin was blue-
puddled snow, I mean
so fine I could trace
your flow from every
tributary. Your breasts,
yes, they were truthful,

freckled and new
beneath your shirt
that summer afternoon
we climbed the ladder
to the barn's dark loft.
We lay down
in the sweet straw
your body
granting the darkness
such mercy
until your brother,
shouting,
brought us down
to fish for crawdads
below the garden.
Your brother,
and your dead sister,
forever between us.
To be with you
I had to pretend
your brother
was my close friend.
On summer nights
we three slept on the lawn
beneath the open sky,
your brother
the dark body
in the center,
we, like wings,
never touching,
unless
I would fling
one arm
in a long arc
across the sky,
perhaps I saw a meteor,
my descending hand
brushing your shoulder,
and you would laugh
and touch my hair
in tender retaliation.
I suppose

you were lonely,
put up with us,
with me
who tugged at you,
innocent and severe,
wanting your skin
to grow around me.
Then your older sister
married and died
within the year.
After the funeral
her husband came for you,
claimed you
from your father
as if you were payment
for that death.
You were sixteen
the day you were taken
by a man in a straw hat
straight-backed
your arms full
of folded clothes
on the front seat
of his car.
I could see everything
from the south pasture
where I lay
tear-shaken, spying
on your leaving,
your solemn descent
from view. I never again
slept with your brother.

Summer Storm

> It's raining cats and dogs.
> —an old saying

i.
Early summer. Our tongues dry up
like sows' dugs. The drought
has turned us from the well
with empty pails.
In the absence of miracles
we pray for the miracle of rain,
remembering the beauty of language,
of Adam giving suck
to names on his tongue.
We dream the language of rain.

ii.
How wonderful to look up
and see them coming,
at first from great distance,
a galaxy of tiny, colored moons
catching the sun,
then see the moons grow
heads, legs, tails,
the shapes of spaniel and bulldog,
the eyes of Siamese and Persian:
a multitude of dogs and cats
tumbling from the sky
in all their ordinary beauty,
reds and browns,
brindles and calicos,
every size and description,
touching, now and then,
little, reassuring caresses,
becoming friends, taking mates,
some giving birth in midair,
kittens and pups, some with wings,
falling from their mothers' wombs . . .

iii.
When we catch them in our arms,
the glistening fur,
the kiss of their tongues,
deep within us something answers,
tells us we are blessed.
Our tongues take up their language.
Our fields lie dark and wet.

Oklahoma Sunset

In the meadow, quail
rattle the beaded grass.

An old man and old woman
nod each other daft.

We listen
to the day's even breathing.

Hives of lilac buzz
in the languorous sunset

the sky's correct
spelling of *evening*.

Woman with Pitcher

How carefully
her hands
describe
the stoneware
pitcher
how it empties
and fills
the stir

of water
inside
a swirl
of shadow
and light
her hands
taking
and giving
the water
forming
its body
as the wheel
turns
as the wet
clay climbs
the pantomime
of her hands.

On the Missouri

i.
Cottonwoods climbing the shore,
plumes of green smoke,
the little corks of fish popping . . .
There is no loneliness like this.
You forget where you came from,
the magic glitter of cities,
the lovely sweat of your loved ones,
the life you had courted and married.
In the steady pulse of the river
you learn patience,
like an old dog
who has learned to stand soberly
above his empty dish
somehow understanding
the unswerving disposition of time.

ii.
In the small towns along the river
we remember these things:
The story the river writes
on the walls of our houses.
How we lived on the roof for three days
and tied the dog to the chimney to save her.
The story of fish.
Where they come to shake your hand.
The quiet gullies of water
where you visit your deaf grandfather,
where you drift to sleep
until he stumbles over your feet
on the way to the kitchen.
Where to knock on water.
And how the mackeral sky, sometimes,
near sunset, is another river.

iii.
If you should leap suddenly into the river
and swim for shore
no one would know
where to forward your laundry
or the names of those who believe you love them.
Only the far shore,
the bluffs like distant relatives,
the trees that will not stop growing,
will answer your call each morning
when you shout *good morning*!
And an old woman,
hunched beneath a cottonwood,
her heavy breasts riding her knees
like two fat babies,
will love you,
even before your teeth fall out,
even before you slip
into the muddy shallows
your tail slapping the water as you swivel.

The Ceremony of the Ducks

>*On the closing of the Peabody Hotel
>Memphis, 1978*

i.
And there was music
in their squawk
and clatter

her laughter
blowing

a white feather
from her lips

as he unbuttoned
the winged collar
of his shirt

his boots sprawled
on the floor
like drunken friends.

ii.
They were
a gift for her

their flutter and walk
each morning
rousing her from dreams.

And he would waken
to her body
feathered in light

her nipples
two notes
on a white page

and to joy
in his own
surprised laughter

as she mimicked
their strut
across the room

her face
over her shoulder

favoring him
with its tiny explosions.

iii.
High above the city
in this Eden
he must leave

each morning
to pay the rent
that he may keep her

she would, barefoot,
walk them to the door,
her sweet babies,

and tie his tie
and kiss his lips.

And could she help
but laugh, watching
that earnest procession

to the elevator
his foolish smile
that took her breath?

iv.
Curled in bed
beneath the morning
drift of light

she closed her eyes
on his way down

and knew his bending
his stroking

those waxy,
skittery backs

like the turn
of her own thighs

the tattoo
of orange beaks
against his legs.

v.
And she remembered
his lifting
the wicker picnic hamper

from the crook
of a street boy's arm
that summer morning

sending
two silver worlds
spinning in sunlight.

Later, spilling
those lively dancers

into her lap
like popped corn!

vi.
She knew
how they would tack
across the lobby,

a tiny flotilla,
swim all day
in the foyer fountain

her lover nearby
in his starched collar

smoothing his moustache
above the counter.

vii.

At dusk
they would return,
her clamorous family,

to chase her laughter
about the room

a snow of feathers
scattering like sneezes

catching
the falling light.

viii.

How well
he loved her

to bring her
such sleek creatures

for her arms
for her breasts

for her white waddle!

The Man Who Would Be a Mother

The stirrings in his chest
are maternal, mild. He imagines
giving suck, the gentle ooze,
the child's lips still forming
around his nipple. He wipes away
the last drop with his thumb,
lifts it to his tongue. Milk.
The first taste in his mouth again.

He would say to his children:
You were once in my belly. This
is how you fed before you were born.
This is where I held you,
child on a rope of blood.
This is my mark on your belly.
When you came into your life,
they held you up for me to see,
as if I were dangling from you, your child.

If I am not your mother,
and you do not rise from my body,
it is not because I would not have it.
Take my hands, as if they were
your face, and when I am dead,
and this flesh unlocks the bones,
imagine birth from my body,
a garden of children blooming.

As She Enters Her Seventieth Year She Dreams of Milk

i.
An early mist
rises

from the mute
curdled brain
of earth

Milk wakens
and speaks
its name

common
as semen

ii.
She remembers
her mother

a white flame
in the dark house

bringing anise
in hot milk

evening prayers
in flannel gowns

her mother bending
above the bed

like a pitcher
pouring

porcelain cups
steaming

their licorice
breath

iii.
And was it
her lover

who knelt
beside her

in the unlit
room

taking
her breast

to his large
face

when she, waking,
felt

the pulse
of milk

within
her chest

iv.
Her husbands
loved

her lush
full breasts

their oyster
mouths

the nipples'
push

against
her blouse

v.
She loved
the mothy sleep
of children

on the slopes
of their fathers

the fish flesh
of wet muzzles

her babies
in their cribs

dream-sucking
the mammal

memory
of milk

vi.
She knows
the tatting

of the cat's
tongue

at the rim
of milk

the blue light
that brims

beneath
the white skin

how milk is grass
and blood

the teeth
of wolves

on clear nights
how the heavens flood

vii.
She knows
how milk comes
and goes

body
the wheel

where babies
turn

how the flesh
will wean

and soon
decay

how nothing
remains

but bone
the stone

of milk
its hard home

viii.
*Old woman
she names
herself*

*heavy
breasts*

*swelling
at her waist*

*like heads
of cheese*

*one more mouth
to feed*

ix.
She bows
her head

and milk
peers up
at her

with its calm
face

The Old Man in His Decline

His sight is gone.
Words sleep before he hears.
He would wake them if he could,
nudge them down the curving throat
of his ear, let them sing again.
Sometimes, that is.

Other times,
he would lie back in his life
as though it were the bed
his mother made for him
when he was young.

He can still see her body,
that tall ship,
sail the dark tides of evening
as he drifts among
the lapped white sheets.

If a man could choose
what to give up, what to keep,
her childhood face would stay,
his babies in his lap
turning their heads like tiny searchlights . . .

Now, as he falls to sleep,
he knows that other presence in his room
that each night breathes more evenly, at peace.

The Other Life

    In this poem
    a man walks along the street
    through a neighborhood of familiar nods,
    extrapolations of trees. In this neighborhood
    there are no sidewalks as stern reminders,
    no salesmen lugging their heavy lives
    door to door. Only windowsills of sanguine
    demeanor, the green addendum of lawn.

    The man pauses at the door
    of a house he will enter. On the couch
    a coat he might have worn, on the rug some slippers.
    From the arrangement of light he knows
    this room has a memory of dear occasions.
    In the kitchen someone has buttered
    toast on a porcelain saucer, set
    a beaded pitcher of milk on the table.

    Those who were once here will be close by,
    children with little tusks of milk pointing,
    a woman sipping butter from the tips of her fingers.
    And when he finds them, those expectant faces,
    those hands folded in laps
    like bows on Christmas boxes,
    he will say, yes, you have done well,
    this is the way it was meant to be.

    And they will be happy, too,
    long years of not knowing behind them,
    knowing now that neither time nor separation
    is the final measure of joy.
    That night, in the various rooms of this house,
    they will kiss each others' lips,
    turn back the thick, dark covers,
    lie down in a solace of possible love.